A HOLE IN THE GROUND
JUST HER SIZE

Lulu Press, Inc
www.lulu.com

ISBN: 978-1-387-70029-5

Any references to historical events, real people, or real places are used fictitiously. Names, characters, and places are products of the authors imagination.

Book design by Leanna Kato

Second Printing Edition 2018

Printed in the United States of America

A HOLE IN THE GROUND JUST HER SIZE

Kelsey Marie Moghadaspour

To those who helped bury me.

And to Lynne for helping me become the young lady I am today.

CONTENTS

TRYING NOT TO LET YOU IN ON MY BREAKDOWN

1.

I feel suffocated–
No, that's not the correct word.
I feel like,
lately, my tear ducts
have been attached to
hoses with no
lack in water supply.
As soon as I get
everything settled,
a bull runs through
my china shop of a mind.

2.

I am not okay.
And you do not seem to
care.

3.

My brain is
an anchor, weighing
me down into my
pillow until it engulfs me whole.

4.

I am my own distraction and
how good is a distraction

when it keeps bringing
up the things that it's
supposed to help you forget?

5.

I have not been okay
for quite some time now.
And still you don't seem to
care.

6.

Not all breakdowns are
loud
and
attention grabbing.
A lot of the time, they're
quiet.

TO THE BOY WHO BURNED ME WORSE THAN I EVER COULD HAVE BURNT HIM

The city skyline mimics the scales that go up and down your back like skyscrapers: dark, sharp, jagged, unloving. Your fingers that I used to hold and caress like they were made of gold, are rotten and sharp. You left cuts on me from when you held me so close, so gently that I didn't realize for months until they scabbed over and it was too late for me to heal them. Those cuts are now scars that crisscross along my body, but nobody can tell the difference between the scars you left on me and the scars I have left on myself. I never realized how much I hated those gnarled and harsh fingers of yours that constantly held a cigarette,

slowly

killing

me.

Your kisses were like burns from the very things you smoked; like when you left a cigarette burn on my finger. Your smoke clouded my life and left me coughing up mucus and blood. You, with your soft brown hair, were a monster I mistook for a genie; a bastard who told me you would grant me my three wishes. You told me you could give me everything I wanted. Instead, you stole a year of my life. A year that will always be tainted with the mixture of your black blood oozing out of every pore, and the mucus from my ever-shriveling lungs.

ODE TO THE PEOPLE WHO HAVE LEFT LIP PRINTS ON MY TIME-LINE

B.B.

You were the first boy I kissed. We went to see *Date Night* in theaters on a "date" with about six other people in middle school and it was awkward and you texted me saying that every time Tina Fey and Steve Carrell kissed, we should kiss. I've heard you're now up there kissing boys and I'm down here kissing a girl so look how that turned out.

R.C.

You shoved your tongue down my throat in a game of spin the bottle while we were on a plane on our way back home from a missions trip. Why did I pine after you for so long?

C.N.

You were my first real boyfriend, and we only dated for a month. I told you I wanted to talk and you got scared and broke up with me over a text so I couldn't break up with you first. Everything was awkward and the first time I saw you after we broke up was when I picked you and our friends up for the parade, and I wasn't told you were going to be there. We didn't kiss until two years after we dated, but you were my New Year's kiss and I don't regret it.

How to Fuck Up A Friendship: A Recipe

One part: awkward glances

Three parts: pressure from friends

Two and a half parts: mistaken tone from text messages

1. Meet at a homecoming dance at a school you don't even go to. You'll exchange glances, and eventually, phone numbers. Blend well for a smooth, average "Junior-Year-in-high-school" relationship.

2. Date for a month; see each other two times in that four-week period. Cut your hair without telling him. Pour into a movie theater and spread evenly for an awkward night where he wasn't invited.

3. Be broken up with over a text. Don't see each other for three months. Become friends again. Put in the oven for two years and check for the perfect amount of sexual tension with a side of a marriage pact.

C.L.

We mostly only ever made out in my car because you didn't have one, and once you did, you totaled it a week later. You always tasted like salami and got a little too handsy. You left for basic training and I got over you. I ended it. You shamed me. We made up. I left for London. You shamed me again.

We're great at this, aren't we?

J.S.

We met on Tinder and you furthered my tea addiction. The first time we met, you worried that I was taller than you because I was wearing my boots. You and your roommate were both potheads and I barely knew what weed was. I kept perfume in my car because even though I never smoked with you, I made sure I didn't smell like it either when I got home. You're back in Ohio and you look pretty happy, for the most part, and I'm happy you're happy. I'm sorry we didn't work out. Your roommate was the one to follow you.

A.J.

Fuck you.

An Equation: Lying to Yourself About Your Feelings

Take **x**. **x** is the boy you can't forget about even though it's been almost two years. Add **y**. **y** represents the underlying anger you have tried so hard to stomp out but to no avail.

x + **y** = you pretending that you don't care anymore so you barely acknowledge him in any of your writing–giving him only two words in a poem about kissing–only to have all of this pent-up anger and no idea what to do with it.

Even math can't help calculate why you left.

A.H.

You made me uncomfortable by coming on too strong, and by "too strong" I mean you pinned me to your couch and tried to make out with me and get in my pants, while watching *Archer*. You were high, and I felt disgusted. I can't watch the first five episodes of *Archer* now because of you. If only I could forget what happened. But there are times when I still feel your hands on my hands, my waist, my everything. When my mum asked me where we had gone for lunch once I had gotten home, and I told her that we went to your apartment, she got mad at me and told me that was a very bad idea. If only she knew that I would never let it get as bad as she was thinking.

N.T.

You were sweet and patient with me. I'm still sorry I made you shave. I feel like I wronged you because while no, I didn't cheat, I was emotionally attached to someone else before our relationship ended. *Does that not count as cheating?*

S.C.

You were the first girl that I kissed who wasn't out of a game of Truth or Dare, or something else equally as idiotic. You were the first to matter.

Cold Hard Truth: And In The End

And even when you've found someone you can see yourself spending the rest of your life with, you still find yourself going back over all of these other people who don't even matter anymore and you realize that you can't fully give yourself to this person who means the world to you because you have so much baggage that the airline won't even let you get on the goddamn airplane.

PRINCESS CHARMING

stop wearing your wishbone where your
backbone ought to be.

fairy godmothers don't appear out
of thin air to grant our wishes and

pumpkins don't turn into carriages and mice
into coachmen. we were raised

on fairytales of how knights in shining armor
will save us and how magic is inside us all. but

I can promise you that the only thing inside
me is hate grown like a weed since

first learning to say the words,
"I can do it myself."

WINGSPAN

they grow from your back
stretching, expanding, filling
the space around you.
shimmery like an
oil spill, the light refracts
off of them, displaying a murky
rainbow.

ERUPTION

I dug myself out of the hole you buried me in. Dirt clogged my lungs and poured from my ears. My eyes were crusted shut.

It took days of picking at the dirt to be functional again. Carving away the pieces that weren't me that you left behind when you buried me. It was days until my eyes could open again and I could see, months until my ears were cleared and I could hear. It was years until my lungs could push and pull the air like I needed them to. Though, they never worked quite like they once did. Now, there's a thin layer of dust that coats the inside of my lungs. Every once and a while dust erupts from my mouth when I speak.

Mother once told me that when you hang around people a lot, you start to become them. I helped you bury me because you wanted me to be you so bad and even now

I'm struggling to find the person I was before.

CHRYSALIS

I buried her.

I tried so hard to make her be like me. Make her into what I knew
would be best for her.
Cocooned her in a bed of dirt.

I went to unearth her. Right where I had laid her to rest.
There was a hole in the ground, just her size.

TOADSTOOLS

Your bed wasn't a real bed. It was a blow up mattress in a storage room of a bedroom in the downstairs of your parents' house. I never slept better than I did that night. I never slept better until I proceeded to work you out of my system, over and over again, because each time I fully purged you, you would resurface and make me feel like hell, all over again.

> I arrived late that night, later than I had intended because I had to maneuver around the truth and my mother. She didn't know I was with you, she thought I was somewhere else. I never lied to her on such a grand scale until I met you. That should've been the first warning.

You pressed your front to my back and my back to your chest. I had ever been held like that before. The dawn light peeked its way into your window just as we were curling up for bed and for the first time in my life, I actually felt wanted and cared for. Like someone thought I was good enough to wrap their arms around. I was eighteen and had barely been kissed. When you held me close, I felt worthy. You would always pop up at my weakest and I think that was the problem; that was when I was so willing to let you back in because I felt alone and unloved.

> You handed me what I was there for and advised that I put it in a peanut butter and jelly sandwich to mask the taste. I shocked you by throwing

them back into my mouth without a second thought. I hated peanut butter and jelly more than I thought I would hate the taste of those, and I was right. All it took was washing it down with an energy drink and I was fine. I smiled at you and you just stood there, mouth agape, for longer than I deemed necessary.

Though nights after that would feel incomplete without the pressure of you behind me, that morning I would periodically awake and kiss your nose, and you would respond by kissing my forehead without even opening your eyes, and you would make me feel like I had finally found something special.

After you were finished being stunned by what I had done, you led me outside to the little set up you had. Your parents' backyard was pretty impressive. The porch was wood with benches installed along both sides. An ivy canopy bridged over the top of us, having help of the wooden guide that arched over the benches. Your hookah sat on the floor of the porch. I eyed it in an uneasy way and you moved it off to the side without saying anything.

Before that, it had been months since you had kissed me. When last we talked about it, you said something along the lines of not wanting me to get the wrong idea. Then you went months without talking to me. You tried so hard to distance yourself from me. And I had let you. I didn't want someone who didn't care about me. I didn't want someone who thought they could use me like a marionette; pull on my strings so I do what you want, throwing me this way and that. But that's exactly what I let you do. Over a year of playing me. Saying you cared about me, I would except your kisses. Then the next day you would send me on a cigarette run for you and when I brought them to your house, you would pretend like I wasn't even there.

> Events unfolded quickly, within the next half an hour. You said I needed to drink a lot of fluids so I wouldn't get dehydrated, so I did. In an instant, everything became humorous. Every time you said something, I would laugh; every time you smiled, I would giggle. Occasionally you would pull out a cigarette and I would go inside to use the bathroom whenever you did. Partially to get away from you and the smoke, partially because I was drinking so much water. Events unfolded quicker–but slower at the same time–after that. The music sang itself slower, began to sound distorted. Suddenly, everything was hilarious. Suddenly, the wood of the deck felt soft. Suddenly, we were on the floor, my head in your lap and your hands in my hair, laughing like we had just discovered what laughter was.

It was soon after that though, you were consistently picking me up from work and taking me to your house. No longer in your parents' house, they had just been in France when you were housesitting. I repaid you in coffee for picking me up from work, and you repaid me for the coffee in kisses. The first one was when we were in your living room, your roommate and your friend were also there. Someone had decided–probably in a stoned state–that we should all watch the Jimmy Neutron movie. I was invested but everyone else's attention span lasted maybe fifteen minutes.

> I believe we were getting close to the peak when the vines told me to tell you they didn't like it

when you smoked and that you should stop. It was cold outside, but I couldn't feel it. You had me wrapped in a blanket and had given me a sweatshirt of yours to make sure I wouldn't feel the sharpness of the night. It was one of the only sweet things you ever did for me. One of the only things that you ever did with good intention. Nothing will compare to that time that I thought you were being kind by letting me try your Funions and then you got mad at me for liking them so much and said something along the lines of, *I told you that you shouldn't try them.*

It didn't take them too long to decide to leave the apartment, for this reason or that, I can't remember. You were laying on the black couch and I sat on the floor, my back to you. Once the room had cleared, and I was still engulfed in the movie, you tapped me on the shoulder. I leaned my head back so I could look at you. You always looked funny to me upside down. Yet, still beautiful. Your jaw wasn't sharp. I couldn't cut myself on it. It was soft, rounded, inviting. I never thought of my jaw as inviting, but you laid your hand to rest on it and held me close. You leaned forward and placed your lips on mine, upside down and all. The kiss was long and soft, and one I may never forget no matter how hard I try to.

I remember looking down at my phone and not understanding what I saw on my screen. I remember opening my texts and trying to send one to a friend that just ended up as a long, incoherent paragraph that I deleted. I remember thinking they were going to worry about me if I didn't text them to tell them that I was okay. I remember not being able to text them. And then I remembered I had told them that I would only text them if something went wrong. My friends worried about me when I was with you–they figured out long before I did that you were bad for me, that I was just your escape from your normal life and that you didn't actually value me in the slightest–and still I couldn't figure out that I should've given up on you long before that.

We began to spend more time than we ever had before together. I met more people that you hung out with–none of them I liked, they were sloppy and rude and they never seemed to remember my name–and you met my family. You were nervous and so was I. But my little brother liked you and used you like a jungle gym and I saw you smile so genuinely that I didn't think anything could go wrong at that point. *How could I, when you looked at someone I loved with so much sun in your eyes?*

Not too much later, I had to use the bathroom again. So, I danced there on my tippy toes. You rolled your eyes but followed me inside. You wanted something to drink. I pirouetted my way down the hallway to the bathroom and did what I had gone in there to do. Your mom had a mirror sitting on the floor, propped against the wall. For some reason, it fascinated me. I sat in front of it and not even ten seconds later I heard you yell from the other room for me not to look at myself in the mirror for too long. When I found you in the kitchen, I asked you how you knew I was looking in the mirror. You told me that most people did their first time. It was a good way to get lost, to make things turn bad. You told me about a time that things turned bad for you and you ended up sitting in an empty bathtub for four hours.

And yet, you started to push me away again. I didn't notice it at first, it took me a while this time. Maybe because I thought we were making progress. I thought you were beginning to trust me with whatever it was you didn't want me involved with before. I finally thought you were trusting me enough to let me in, into the mess that you decided you were. You said you weren't worth it, but wouldn't that have been my decision to make? I still wish I would've listened to you the first time. You stopped responding to me as often, you didn't pick me up from work as much as you had been.

Time passed and didn't. I was coming down and lightning shot across the sky, making me feel as if it had shot through me, leaving me vapid and lifeless on the bench on your parents' back porch. Eventually–at about six in the morning–we made our way downstairs to your storage room of a bedroom and got into bed. I never slept better than I did that night and I wish I never thought about that night anymore.

We've gone in circles–over and over again–since we first met and I have finally made my way out of your orbit but you occasionally keep trying to nudge your way into my universe. Every attempt you've tried has failed and I couldn't be more proud of myself for keeping you out.

FLOODED ARE THE LANDS I CALL MY HOME

In The Beginning – Adam Ybarra

In the begi–
There
was
nothing.

Rocks rise from the ground.
Trees canopy over,
weaving their way through
my mind as I make my way
to the water bank.

Jagged ground trips me,
cuts my knees.
Cuts my tongue;
teeth clenched,
copper fills.

In the beginning
there was me.
I knew nothing
but solitude.
There has never
been anyone else.

Greenery flows,
disguising the land.
Greenery chokes
the air around me.
Leaving me with no room–
no space to breathe.

The river escapes.
Flooding the bank,
the rocks,
my home,
my mind.

I hide under my
rock that protrudes
from the ground.
There is so much
space out there,
so much sky staring
back at me.

In the–
I had nothing.
In the beginning
nothing
meant
anything.
In the beginning

I was left
with my thoughts,
all of which have
floated away.

CHILD OF THE FOREST

The earth is my home.
I was born from the ground,
pulled out of a creature
    I had yet to know;
    dirt surrounded me like a cradle,
    leaves kept me covered.

Gooey, dirty, and wrapped in leaves.
Some sniffed at me. Others tilted
    their heads.
They didn't know what I was.
They didn't know where I came from.

I learnt to crawl from the help
    of caterpillars.
I walked side by side with
    wolf cubs as my company.

My skin perpetually had
    one
    two
    three
    layers of forest.
My hair was matted,
    strong as bark.

As I grew, I knew my forest

as well as any of the creatures
who also resided there.

I knew which tree held which
family and I knew how to
find the river with just
a whiff of the air.

The trees flowed through
every shade of green imaginable.
The air was thick and clung to me
as I cascaded through the canopies
and the treetops.

When I was weak,
they made me strong.
They taught me to hunt
so I would always have food.

They gave me everything
I ever needed.
What they didn't provide for me,
the forest did.

Until the day I tried to leave.

I wanted to see more,
to know more.
I wanted to see what
I could find.

So I tried to leave.
Little did I know,
the forest didn't like goodbyes.

Little did I know,
that so many years ago,
shrouded by dirt and leaves,
the forest claimed me.

I tried to walk away,
but as soon as I did,
my skin began to bubble.
White hot pain traced its way
through my body.

Bulbous lumps took up residence on
my arms
my legs
my back.
From them sprouted vines that
whipped through the air
finding handholds on a
nearby tree.
They pinned me to its bark
and wound their way
back and forth.

Soon, I was a part of that tree.
Unable to move, unable to leave.

I had become one with the forest
and the forest refused to
lose me.
So it cocooned me,
entombed me in a tree.

I was a child of the forest,
and the forest loved me.

REMEMBRANCE

The vines vibrated and cooed,
wrapping their tendrils around me,
giving me the love I always wanted.

They show me the love I crave
like an addict, what I want from the bleeding
heart next door, before I realize
I would never receive it.

A LATE NIGHT CONVERSATION WITH SEARCH ENGINES

search: how do i tell my mother im not lazy im just depressed

did you mean: how to explain something to someone who doesnt understand

search: what are symptoms of bipolar disorders

did you mean: am i going crazy

search: why didnt they care

did you mean: why do i still care

LANDFILL

Many have come

and gone

and I am here,

alone. There is no one

for me to exist with.

They claim to

be here forever,

but they don't

know the meaning

of forever like I do.

WORK OF ART

you are a canvas, paint
splayed all over,
abandoned by
the people who left
their marks on you.
you are a tapestry, thread
through the ringer.
you have been poked
and prodded and
are still in progress.

COLORED DAYS

Red days are days that neither of us want.
Red like that time you shoved the couch in anger.
Red like my face once I had finished yelling.
Red like the siren that appeared behind us, conjured from nothing.
The days where either of us are red with anger or stupidity because of something asinine.

Grey days are the days when I feel numb and you don't know what to do so I feel
bad and you feel like a failure.

Blue days. Those are the days when almost anything can make me cry.
And you get frustrated because I'm dysfunctional.
(I would be frustrated too.)
But blue is your favorite color,
so I hate to equate it to something
so negative.

Green days are quite wonderful, actually.
Green days are the days we spend
outside.
Like in Florida, that night when we went swimming in the ocean,
and you kissed me, tasting like salt water
and sunscreen, and you told me that you
loved me.

Or when you took me to the Japanese Garden
 while we were in Houston, because you knew it would
 make me happy.
Or that night when we went on that long walk and it was dark
 and that dog startled us.

The uneventful days, they're orange.
They aren't really spectacular, one way
 or the other.
They're mediocre days.
No fighting.
No outstanding memories.
Nothing worth writing home about.

Yellow days are probably the happiest, because who doesn't
 equate yellow
 to happiness.
They're bright and shining,
 like your face when
 we've just woken up in the morning
 and you're looking at me
 and you're grinning like no other.
Or my face when you've just walked in the door from work
 and I haven't gotten to see you all day.

But while yellow days may be the happiest or shiniest,
 purple days are classified under
 favourites.
Purple like that night we stayed out
 talking until five in the morning and
 I didn't end up going to sleep at all.
 So I stayed up to watch the sunrise with the bunnies
 and you wished you had too.
Purple like that time I didn't feel well

and you showed up at my door
with my favourite flower and
favourite drink in hand and
you didn't leave
until the morning after.
Purple like our first night in our first rental together
when we hadn't seen each other in two months and
I was too tired and too lazy to put sheets on my bed
and you rolled your eyes at me and made us sleep
in your bed instead.

FLORA

Me, a daffodil. Narcissistic with no care for another.

My mother is a jasmine, full of romance and so beautiful.

Narcissus, I am treasured by both the king

and the queen of the underworld. I am revered,

trembled before. And yet, nothing

I do outshines her compassion

and her love.

HALLOWEEN

The first Halloween we spent together was during our junior year of high school. You arrived without costume and our friends and I reamed you for it; a white t-shirt, a pair of jeans, and a jacket that donned your school's logo. I dressed as a character from one of my favorite books and you, of course, didn't know who it was. That was okay.

We trick-or-treated the night away, and eventually the sky soaked us to the bone so we were forced to retreat and regroup in my living room. We all hauled up with our candy and watched whatever Disney Channel Halloween movie was on television. Because what else were a bunch of sixteen and seventeen year olds supposed to do on a holiday that was marketed more for a younger audience?

The next day, you invited me over after dinner to watch a movie and you let me choose what we ended up watching. So, I sat down on your living room floor, your movie collection sprawled out in front of me, and I ended up choosing *Wreck-It-Ralph*, which you still give me shit for, saying how it's not a good date movie.

We sat on your couch and watched it, just us two. Legs intertwined and somehow never disturbed by your four other family members. Whatever you had told them to make sure they didn't intrude, I don't know what it was but it apparently worked. Because between coming in and meeting everyone, and you asking your mom to give me a ride home, I didn't see or hear a soul in that house.

Before she drove me home, you asked me to be your girlfriend and if you could kiss me. I said yes to the first and no to the second. I wasn't ready for that quite yet. I could only take so many butterflies in one night.

Your mom dropped me off. With one slip of my key into the door, I was inside my own home. Where I felt safe and could finally let myself sigh and let the awkwardness I had been feeling all evening wash over me.

"Kim, is that you?" I heard my mom call for me from the kitchen.

"Yeah mom, it's me." I hung my jacket and keys on their hook in our entryway and slipped off my shoes before tossing them into the basket my OCD mother decided was something we needed.

She appeared out from behind the wall that held our pantry, something that was a mix of a smile and a smirk played at her lips. "So, how'd it go at Colton's?"

I shrugged; I could feel the anxiety that at the time I had mistaken for butterflies rising in me again at being asked about my evening. "It was fine. He asked me to be his girlfriend."

My mom beamed. I had never dated anyone before. "Oh, honey, that's great! I'm so happy for you!" She came over and wrapped her arms around me. I buried my face in her shoulder, with hopes that the lingering anxiety I had would trickle away.

I joined her in the living room to finish whatever she had

been watching, the rest of the family already having gone to bed. She sat on the couch and I took up residence on the floor. After about twenty minutes or so of this, I asked something that was on my mind.

"Hey mom, how do you feel about helping me cut my hair really short?"

She paused the show she was watching and finished the bite of food that was in her mouth. "I mean, we could definitely do it. You know I'm a fan of your long hair, but you're old enough to make that decision for yourself. You should ask Colton first though, before you do anything."

I made a face and leaned back on my arms, "Why should I ask Colton first?"

"Because that's what you do when you have a boyfriend."

That was four years ago.

The next Halloween was spent apart; on two different sides of the world, and in the fact that we were no longer dating and hadn't been since the end of November that past year. I was in a hostel in some country in Europe, drinking strawberry daiquiri's and eating cake provided by a denim company who was celebrating their tenth year being in existence. You were home, spending it with our friends but lacking in me. Part of me wished I could be home with the ones I knew. Part of me really didn't care.

For three months surrounding that holiday, I was traipsing all around Europe, seeing whatever I could see. Though I never did stop talking to you and the rest of our friends.

Even when I missed homecoming with you all, you guys

attempted to FaceTime me so it was like I was still there. Though for you it was too loud to hear anything and for me it was four in the morning and I was really tempted to try and use my non-existent mind powers to murder you all through the phone. The thought behind it was sweet and had commenced because you all were missing me so I called off the mind powers and let you all live. I would've been too lonely once I returned home if I had followed through with it anyway.

We played with this back and forth interest. I was the person that once they were away from the thing that was always in question, they thought that was what they wanted. I thought you were what I wanted. It was a mess and nothing came of it except broken expectations and maybe a little bit of heartbreak. I was always the one to be setting up expectations that I never followed through with, and you were always the one that was left to pick up the pieces of their own heart. I think this is where we discovered that we work better as friends and not as an item, as much as we maybe wanted to be one.

That was three years ago.

Our third Halloween was then spent together again. Fresh out of the hospital and still on the weaker side of existence, I couldn't do a lot, which ruled out the normal Halloween activity of trick-or-treating. You were dressed as a cop–or your future career, however you think it's best to word–and I was a faun. We were with our friends Minnie Mouse, a zombie, and one who wore a pink and black polka-dotted onesie and a tiara, just because he could. We played Cards Against Humanity and drank cider's that I had smuggled up to Minnie's bedroom awkwardly in a backpack–praying that they didn't break–so that her parents wouldn't see. Some could've called that evening boring but I think it still is one of my favorite Halloweens to date.

It was weird doing anything even remotely normal that year because we had all graduated high school and were doing our own things. Minnie came back from college for the weekend to spend it with us, and I had just deferred my acceptance to the university that took me in from the cold. You were waiting to leave for the Marine's and we were sad all that you were going.

Before I left in January we spent as much time together as we could, going on our normal, late night Taco Bell runs where we would sit in your car in the parking lot and make up scenarios of us being cops together, but it still wasn't enough when I think about it now. I even went to work out with you a few times, always hating myself a little bit afterwards, and I never did that for anyone.

We would sit in front of my house on the sidewalk, legs splayed out into the road, the only things illuminating us being the streetlights and my garage light, and we would talk about everything and nothing until it was three in the morning and I had accidentally gotten locked out of my house.

This time we didn't play at the idea of being together even remotely. Both of us with our deep-seated feelings and our lack of confrontational skills instead declared a marriage pact: if we were both single at the age of 35, then we would get married in a best friend holy union and spend the rest of our lives annoying the absolute shit out of one another. It went down in my history as the most important pinky promise I have ever made, to this day. It's something I still have tucked safely away in my heart.

That Halloweem, after everyone had parted ways, you offered to walk me down to my house, even though it was just at the end of the street. Buzzed off the ciders and the fun we had just had, I was feeling joyous and full of love.

"Hey," I bumped you with my hip, "you know you're super important to me, right?"

You shrugged and said something along the lines of, "Nah, I'm not super important to anyone. I rolled my eyes. I wasn't in the mood for your self-deprecating jokes.

"Seriously. You're my best friend, and I don't know what I'd do without you."

"Good, because you're not going to get rid of me that easy."

I chuckled, "Who said anything about getting rid of you at all?"

You smiled and wrapped your arm around my shoulders. We made it to my house rather quickly, but instead of going inside, we sat on my porch. I stared off into space for a minute, and was only brought back because you had started to talk.

"What do you think it would be like if we ever got married?"

I answered without hesitation, "I think we would be the grandparents our family would hate to invite for holidays, but would feel obligated to. You'd be the old war veteran, always muttering about something and diving behind furniture, and I'd be the drunk grandma that would just yell at you as my voice slurred."

You were laughing before I even finished, "'Back in my day, we didn't have it so cushy!'" You imitated your aforementioned old self. I was laughing so hard I couldn't even contribute.

"You know what, we should have a marriage pact. Because obviously, we would be great. We would raise the best kids." You laughed, but agreed. "It's settled then! When we're thirty-five, or so, if we're both single, we will get married. And it'll be the best best-friend marriage this world has ever seen!" I held out my pinky.

"Agreed." You twisted your pinky around mine and it was set in something better than stone.

That was two years ago.

The next two Halloween's were spent away from each other, forming something we had yet to see; you were in the military and I was in school. Each passed without much significance. It was weird to not spend it with you. Or anyone I had known for longer than a year. Both years we both worked Halloween; you with what you were always doing nowadays, being pulled this way and that by the military; me at the mall, handing candy out to children and wanting to pound my head into the wall due to the severe number of children that never seemed to stop.

Our orbits were weird, crashing into each other in our weakest moments. Even now still, though we're both happily, not-really-engaged, and still I sit here and beat myself to death with the *what if?* that encompasses our whole past and future.

That was last year. And this year. Because we're getting to that point in our lives where routines start to form and there is no way to avoid this.

LAUNDROMAT

Baby blue walls and
folding stations from the 80's.
Retro chairs line the walls
awaiting the spines of today's
attendees to watch the
internal struggle of
whether or not to
forget or hold on tight.
Memories are washed away
in these machines.
The smell of him,
gone from your sheets
from the night before.
The wine stain from her glass
that she threw in your face.
You tell yourself it's for the best,
that you can't spend anymore
time or energy crying for them.
Wishing they would come back
and crawl into your arms.
Wishing you could tell them

how you feel.
Tell them how you messed up,
how you wish they were still there
with you, how you think of them
every day.
And then you move on,
you repeat the cycle of heartbreak.

PULLING STRINGS

legs splayed like a strung-up puppet
forced to dance the dance
lower limbs coiled around each other

contorting and conforming
given only a moment for breath
before the strings are pulled taut

expected to perform again
no pause long enough
for a sip of water

washed in black and white
the important things
bleached and sundried

the parched and dried up organs
snapping and dissolving
at the lightest pull

the clicks of splintered lifeless limbs
broken time and time again
never given the phase to mend

the grey matter mind
rotten and reeking
leaking out an ear

and down a cheek
waiting to hit the linoleum
just below

SEA MAIDEN

My name means Dweller at a Ship Island. I am the ship island, luring boats closer and closer until I drown them in my waters. Dark, cold, relentless; I am the storm that pushes you to me for shelter. Both the safety you feel, and the nightmare that paralyzes you, I am the enigma that may never be solved. Larger than life, but made smaller by those who disparage me. I am the waves; full of power and crashing down onto my shores where I collect things from the oceans surrounding me. Humans throw their sorrows into the sea; broken engagements, heartbreak, the death of a loved one, the dreams they once had that crashed down around them. And they float, all alone, in the water for me to find. Small treasures, they are. My only taste of the human lives that are just past my shores. For I have exposed all that I am worth with nothing to show. I have broken my back time and time again to collect these small human treasures. So be wary. Get caught in my currents, try to take my gems from me, and I will show no mercy.

SELF PORTRAIT

She is a mirror,
with the solar system exploding on her arm, as fiery as ever, always threatening to consume her whole, leaving nothing behind except those she has loved.

She is a mirror,
with ever-changing hair–similar to her feelings; blue like the unexplored depths of the ocean, purple like the deepest line of royalty, brown like the soil she dares tread upon.

She is a mirror,
adorned in jewels and pleasantries that she uses to distract those from seeing her meager existence.

She is a mirror,
with pen and paper in hand, ready to note the inspiration blooming around her, but never knowing the correct order for words she has yet to find.

She is a mirror,
scared to let people in–let them see the real her–so she locked the doors tight that not even the wind could reach her. But you must have majored in lock picking because you are like Monet with a bobby-pin.

She is a mirror,

she reflects everything back to you. No part of her is genuine; she is made up of bits and pieces of thousands of different people in her lifetime.

I HAVE WRITTEN

I have written so much
about the same thing
that the majority
of it is just repeating,
repeating, repeating.

I have written
love poems
hate poems
excuses.

I have written you
into my head
and I have written
myself
under the table.

I have written myself
onto the page so now
you can consume me
whole.

I have written myself
out of my body
for you to see
and for me
to fade away
because why would you need
two of me?

INCARNATE

The earth has crusted
Over and I finally
Am on my way out.

ACKNOWLEDGEMENTS

I just wanted to take a minute to give thanks to all those who have helped me along my way.

Firstly, I would like to thank my parents. Mom, you've always done what you could to further the artist in me and support me in my craft. Dad, you created the need for travel in my life that still has yet to be satisfied (let's hope it forever stays insatiable). Rick, you've been around longer than I can even remember and you've done so much for me. Nothing I ever say or do will fully express how thankful I am. Becky, you may not have helped raise me, but you've already done so much for me. Thank you all so much, I love all of you to the moon and back.

Next, to Alex, Cameron, Courtney, Kendra, Mia, and all of my other friends who have supported my writing and me since we met: thank you all so much, from the bottom of my heart.

To Lynne, to being the best life group leader a young girl could have. For always being there for me and helping me see which way was up. Rest in peace.

To Leanna Kato, thank you for encapsulating my book and designing the perfect cover.

Thank you to Anne, James, Julia, Matt, Michael, and Quintan for being amazing professors and always pushing me to do my best.

And last but not least, thank you to Sara, for always supporting me and giving me a hand to hold when I need it most.

www.ingramcontent.com/pod-product-compliance
Ingram Content Group UK Ltd.
Pitfield, Milton Keynes, MK11 3LW, UK
UKHW040557210726
13854UKWH00007B/1374

9 781387 700295